Solar Cruise

Claire Crowther

Solar Cruise
a memoir

Shearsman Books

First published in the United Kingdom in 2020 by
Shearsman Books Ltd
PO Box 4239
Swindon
SN3 9FN

Shearsman Books Ltd Registered Office
30–31 St. James Place, Mangotsfield, Bristol BS16 9JB
(this address not for correspondence)

www.shearsman.com

ISBN 978-1-84861-692-9

ACKNOWLEDGEMENTS

Thanks to *The Fortnightly Review, The Next Review, Poetry Wales*
and *London Review of Books* for publishing some of these poems.

I would like to thank the many people who have helped progress these poems
especially the Helyar Poets: Fiona Benson, Patrick Brandon, Julia Copus,
Jane Draycott, Annie Freud and Jenny Lewis. Most notably I must thank the
Stockwell Poets who have read the entire ms: Anne Berkeley, Sue Rose, Siriol
Troup, Tamar Yoseloff. A very special thanks to Ian McEwen for his regular
critiques, to Julith Jedamus for her insights, to Linda Black for always
knowing what I'm talking about and the deepest gratitude to Carrie Etter
for her encouragement, textual guidance and being thereness.

As to being there, my family never fail me and, lastly, my thanks are not
enough for my partner, Keith Barnham, who is the subject of *Solar Cruise*.
Our planet is also grateful.

CONTENTS

for Keith Barnham

'Physics is S.S. Eschatology.'
Hurtle B Hurtle, www.blogspew.com

'Where are the small experimentalists?
Where are the cellar labs and the string
and the three a.m. light burners? I'm
not saying no expertise. I'm looking for
shabby. Are all the science professionals
shiny nowadays? Is it all conferences and
TV shows? We need savers not ravers.'
 @FloodsUpGals: The Underhyping of
Climate Change

A Conference Dinner Takes the Future on Board – *in my view*

Once-powerful dock. Historic boat:
the *S.S. Eschatology.*
Sweet talk, run softly till the feast is over.

> *– meet the particle physicists, funded for findings in *Rapture Physics, and waiting out the End Times, defining small matter. The marvels of nano-beginnings, debris of the first particle, gleam and go in the shy firefly Higgs boson.*

So when an old solar physicist
stands up, in shrunken jeans, sandals,
and says, 'All we need are extravert bosons,

streams of golden photons that will free
new current. Leave the Higgs to hide…'

> *– of course, there is no applause. Sir Olkincole shakes a corporate, corporeal hand among the suits.*

But my old physicist's emerald forest flourishes:

crystal-quick cells, experimental
leaves, threatened species. If one bee
should soar to swarm and undulate and carry

time to change … one student stands. She claps.
She barefaces fuss.

> *Future: you brim with data for us.*

The Power of Gold

Our parents prospered, worked,
pensioned. Their kids haven't shirked

whistling through oscillating corridors, half in tune
with a baby grand. Chopin

is cooling off in the Carinthia lounge. Outside
waves glitter and collide

> *with hubris. Am I not different to
> all dead poets as my physicist to dead
> physicists?*
>
> *I write crosswise. I experiment with
> words.*

He works on the power of gold
 photons to keep us warm.

Harvest in the Quantum Well Solar Cell
Reminds Me of Lipstick

'Look,' my physicist says. I look.

There: a speck of disc
in his palm. 'Cheaper
cleaner fuel. No
more nuclear waste.

> *Red Hazard*

No more stink of oil

> *Cursed Purple*

with this crystal: gall-
ium arsenide
quantum well solar cell:

I keep it on me.
Here,' he says. I hear:

> *Sunstalkin*

Keith's Hand With Cell

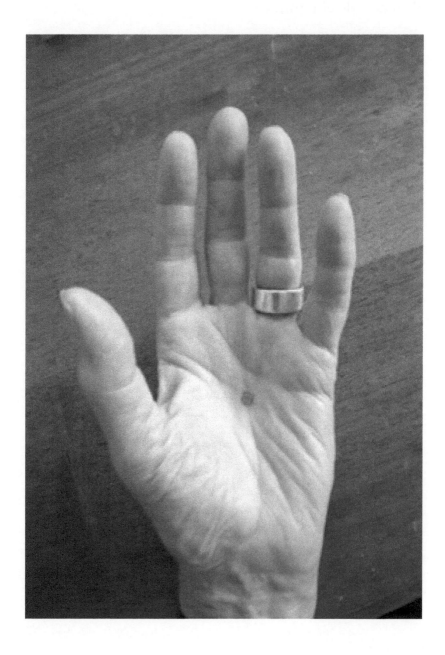

Heart Cut Out of the Sun

A quantum well, a speck,
lies heartlike on his palm.

I make out such a shape
through a body of time:
my gran's good Brummie heart,
dismembered from the Rhine
and also, tabloid grey,
a photo years have blanched,
meat on a murderer's table,
a heart dished up for lunch.

That newsprint, ample, grand
on her settee, has cooked,
like rhubarb I had cloaked
in crockery to grow,
sour in me. She bound
covers for better books.

His heart beats on his hand
and I will cover it.

Foghorn with Solar Harvester

Beneath and around his palm
on which balances one possible future
the Atlantic
calms
and swells.

A sheen of fog curtains our balcony
and into that the captain sends a throaty

ohhhhm

ohhhhm

ohhhhm

This Is the Question

During the voyage we share
        lyrics / lyric
        physics / physic

We talk about the consequences
        of the answer to one question:
to say or not.

'I choose to say,' my physicist says.
'What's your decision?'

'Here,' I say. 'These words.'

A Short History of CERN* by Two Physicists

1 A PARTICLE CHASER'S SOLILOQUY

Why am I here?
To build an upside down duomo.

To shaft through Jura rock.

> *On Lowering Day, someone dropped a*
> *spanner.*
> *It missed tons of sinking machinery.*

To command a yard of copper wire
down here among the orange hard hats.

To monitor the silver pipe. It beams
protons that smash themselves and make
new particles.

> A nanosecond later,
another crash, more bunches of new beings.

To find which particle is which.
To hunt the Higgs boson through beam-born bits,
as many people as live in North America.

> *It's so shortlived, it's never been*
> *seen live.*

To saddle sunlight,

to smack the flanks of photons and send up
data to where a thousand computers stare
down through their sweating floor to the pantheon.

To name what's been particularised.

> *Why, how light a thing a boson can be:*
> *a weightless waving string of photons,*
> *that hit our retinas, wake us*
> *to the multiplicity we call nothing.*

There they play, bosons of zero mass
while Higgs lurks, heavy, invisible.

To tell its resurrection,
to do so together.

11 THE RAREST PARTICLE

My physicist left CERN halfway through his career. There would be no more researching the world's first moments as a high priest of Rapture Physics once, on CERN's preprint library shelves, he'd found David Mathisen's 1979 thought experiment testing the world's last moments.

Not that a Rapture denier might not share some qualities with a Rapturist: vision, dedication, a conviction that he has theorised the Truth and only needs to get it into service. The Professor, my experimental physicist, is a natural rapturist. The difference is that his rapture will be the gathering up of humans into the mortal future of the earth rather than their gathering up into the immortal extinction of their species.

One hundred years to the day that Einstein was born, one paper by David Mathisen, an unknown but Sibylline physicist, delivered my physicist to his mission. That the world could be lost was not new but to frame time with that supposition, to give it dates as Mathisen had done, led him to think that he could interact with the process of human eschatology. And so he escaped the Rapturist's delusion that The Catastrophe cannot be avoided. He framed the experiment of a saved world.

The Triptych of Power

i The Chosen One

when one golden photon from a sunbeam
lights up a crystal solar cell
it gives all of its energy to one of the cell's electrons

ii The People

though many electrons hold the crystal solar cell
the chosen electron rises
and creates a positron from each electron's rib
which frees them all
unexpectedly
and thus together
they make electricity

iii Coincidence of Crystal

a chosen electron needs to power its cohort
with the amount of energy
delivered by one golden photon.

A Prayer at the Foot of the Page

Sunlight! star cast,
we are your kind.

After Dinner Speaker

*We are in the Carinthia Lounge, a lounge
named after a ship long scrapped but famous
for the sailors' strike caused by passengers
complaining that deckhands played skiffle
music in their off hours.*

When he takes on others making the crossing
through this treeless passage,
when he conjures the concept of artificial leaves,
the others think his anaphora is anathema.
I cower. He does not:

'The artificial leaf   is   one more source of fuel
The artificial leaf   is   a metaphor for the real leaf
The artificial leaf   is   developed by the scientific method*
The artificial leaf   is   less complicated than the real leaf

*thus cutting short
   the half billion years nature took
        using CO_2 and sunlight
            to perfect a breath-enabling growth fuel.'

Give that man a ukelele.

The Patroniser

I cannot watch the dire
Sir Dogrel Olkincole,
or some such, shake his fist,
urge the dress suits and lace
          to beware scientists.

'The artificial leaf produces ethanol, are you saying?'
'The artificial leaf can't produce pure alcohol yet but, yes…'
'Want to get drunk on your own roof, eh? Moonshine!'

Sir Olkincole's sweet wife
pats my hand and murmurs,
"Never mind. He doesn't
          really mean it. Really."

In the Ship's Library

I order a fresh mint tea,
stand near the leather arm chair
above a kneeling passenger,

and remain absent to someone who hasn't come,
who is not there, who has made different
decisions, who laughs
about messed up arrangements,

and urges me not to get lost down decks –
which I have, reading this:

Abstract

In the 1930s Ernest Rutherford (1871–1937)
repeatedly suggested, sometimes angrily,
that the possibility of harnessing atomic energy
was "moonshine".

Yet, as war approached he secretly
advised the British government
to "keep an eye on the matter."

I suggest that Rutherford did not really believe
his "moonshine" claim,
but did have profound reasons for making it.

If I am correct, then this casts additional light
on his personality, stature, and career.

Moonshine in Memoriam

Let's not delay the light –
the sunflare, sunshine, sundazzle in quantum's soul.

Genia in Memoriam:
Irène Joliot-Curie, Ida Noddack, Lisa Meitner

The first person to suggest that the nucleus of an atom could split in two parts and two of the leading experts in the analysis of the resulting debris were women.

Irony 1: Gender Fission

you could say the Great Bomb was delayed
by men who couldn't sit
with women first explaining
how an atom splits

Irony 2: The History of the Waist by Lisa Meitner Who Famously
Described the Splitting Atom as Waisted

A man does not have a waist.
He has a midriff. A middle.

He also has a belly and a breadbasket,
a paunch, pot and general girth.

A woman has a waist.
A woman has been required to identify her waist.
A woman gains a neutron to do this.
A man remains a spherical uranium nucleus.

A woman has been deemed
beautiful in the absence of
a deep breath,
but a woman becomes
explosive when a waist of
energy is imposed upon her.
She splits.

Irony 3:
I Gain Confidence in the Ocean Metaphor Dominating This Book

Lisa Meitner
pictured
a nuclear explosion
as a drop
of water breaking

a simile of sea
volatile wet land

and her image of this invisibly small break
unlike Tennyson's whole grand sea
breaking, breaking,
breaking on its cold grey stones...

Irony 4

...inspired Enrico Fermi,
the unwaisted physicist,
to split the atom in Chicago
under a squash court.

No Irony Here

Noddack and Meitner, your comments please:

Being wasted researchers,
when we surmised what would happen
when the atom split,
we didn't suppose we would get the Nobel prize
and we didn't.

I did.   *(Irène J-C)*
My name, maybe?

The Ghost of Marie Curie Works Up a Chorus while Chatting to Enthusiasts at a Model Engine Rally in 2015

All you men crouching by a nine-carriage train
that's stopped sauntering through the countryside, I know
you dream that what you've made will move again.
I know why you stay stooping

over cream and maroon livery when stock
rolls out of Gorpeton Blimey. You are checking
lost detail. You'll remake exactly what
you've made. Your trains are guarding,

circling, what was engineered long since. For once,
turn away from Bassett-Lowke traction engines,
read this ad for radium – *Buy a Piece*
Through the Post! Experiment!

Model Engineering knew in 1910
a woman had found what none of us could have made.
When I identified rays
that move through fog, through flesh, through fact, after

I'd ground, dissolved, collected precipitate,
I stunned a moment. Steam,
with its air of work and modernity – lost.
Oh, you've reconstructed my front-line X-ray cars!

They were nicknamed *les petites Curies*. They drove
away old views: perfect toys for discovering
the location of shrapnel
in bodies (broken, but they moved again.)

My Raver

How did my physicist find out
quantum wells could change
working solar cells, could give us
more light? Till then, nobody
had thought of such a thing. So, many
colleagues thought he must be raving.

Still, some minds were changed eventually.
Still, the problem of prematurity in physicists
needs recognition.

The First Criticisms Every Solar Sceptic Makes Drive a Physicist-loving Poet to Doggerel

'Solar is unpredictable. We don't get much sun!'
'No. It peaks near noon.
You'll keep your oven on.'

'How can wind be solar?'
'Offshore and onshore
the sun blows by the hour,

and bioelectricity is
made from sun: waste
is fuel. So is piss.'

Are We Wasting Our Time?

Our rocking sea
is floor and ground and base and shoe, and I
am not sure
footed on it. I might not get over
to our future though I row, row, row, row, row
in my head, in my middle ear that lies
between one hair and another, sickening,
constantly whispering,

                                    the voyage
                    is wrong and you are wrong and he is wrong
                                    and sea is not stability.

Sea's built right,
but I am not a rower and I would not.

The Crystallier: A Memoir in Which
I Fable the Sociopolitical Side of Science

And in that disused lifeboat, the gods held a party.
Living saints attended.

At this rave, the God of Poetry, Brigid,
tripped over the snoozing God of Physics, Electron,

and begged him to deal with his boredom
since bosons are not trash.

The music of the spheres still taxed her.
So Electron lied: 'OK, right, I'm on it.'

Before drifting off again, he nudged my physicist
who, at that moment, was asleep himself

sagging over a table in the library at CERN
after a long shift attending the accelerator

and he woke from his weird dream of a rave
knowing that he must create a crystal for a low-energy future.

From decade to decade Brigid checked
that Electron had been on it

and Brigid gave credit to Electron's push of shy crystal researcher
into righteous deliverer of properly resourced outcomes.

Thus was my physicist received with joy in a few desolate marinas.
Brigid agreed with that good-time god, Electron,

that there should be a lyric outcome.
not for immortality, which the gods already have,

(electrons don't die ever)
but for mortals whom the gods seem to want to impress at parties.

Thus in the final tired hours of our world-saver voyage
I relax for an hour or two and dream of a Crystallier

> *and of Brigid*
> *who will transcribe this history*
> *into the Collection Celestial.*

On Not Being a Fish Given the Sea's Proximity

Back in the cabin, for a hard dance of work,
he calls on me, a non-scientist, to think.

I move my computer to our balcony
with its two plastic chairs and no windows.

Rainy wind on the muscular arm of rail.
He says, 'Metaphors are equations:

each side of the equals sign   is   an image that coincides
with one on the other side   and   the whole phenomenon inheres one truth
          or two

$$E = hf$$

$$E \qquad = \qquad hf$$

this describes the nature of sunlight as billions of photons

and of the digital camera
and of the mobile phone
and of the silicon chip
and of the computer
and of the e-book

and of the solar cell.'

And, after perhaps an hour, thinking of pagan marriage at sea, I force out this thought:

'wE   are the same as   the **handfasted**.'

Marriage, a Sunbeat

Don't we feel the natural sound of sun
      beating inside itself as any human body beats?

Don't our atoms measure disruption
      into unexpected lines or graphs as we float on?

Do we take ourselves to heart
      and resonate?

Are we all Antarctic ice sheets cracking
      in weakening heat, singing under strain?

Surely the sun gives us our physic.

Wingding

While rude sea rides
Arse up down tit
Hurly hugger
Burly mugger
Hurry helter
Scurry skelter

Ocean notions
Of commotion
Dupli- and
Reduplicating
See saw sea sighs
No land stirs just

This soft toiler
Spoiler country
We float on fret
Rude and rowdy
It's our party
Drinking carbon

Sun shines in
Our deep devices
Some part water
Some tread on it
There's a scar-
City of prophet.

Denied Confirmed: the News Gnomic

one-eyed squirmed

secretive   nuclear facility

beguiled conformed

meteorological   late September

demised infirmed

radioactive isotope ruthenium -106   atmospheric

descried informed

accident

seniled alarmed

986 times the norm

termed defied

not linked

to reassure

well below

20,000 times less

sighed concerned

no threat

Confession of Two Introverts

We ignore
the wired floor
of the sea:
No Facebook, no Twitter,
no Instagram, no WhatsApp.
We don't dredge those depths

for which the small room
on a lower deck
is crammed with computers.
A harassed aide de media sits at a desk,
assisting the shivering e-lost
and the e-lonely
to get their virtual oxygen
and go underwater.

We're thinking here, don't disturb us,
you siren voices, calling:

> *O physicist, O poet*
> *your numbers don't add up,*
> *we don't know what you mean,*
> *we don't like your work,*
> *why don't you rest?*

Even if there were windows in the media room,
we would not go there.

She Counts, He Counts

I am becalmed
more than halfway
perhaps almost
all of the way

along my life.
Berth unto berth,
country to land,
wife to husband.

I can't tell which
equational
side I hold or,
loosening thread,

what ship or land
would sink beneath
the rising sea
if he lost me?

Syllabic shapes
have the pattern
of my stanzas,
as scientists

are patterned by
their fields. Tapping
my knee all through
our talks. Counting.

Counting. Counting
syllables. Tick
through sentences
airing futures.

Futures called out
and stood up for.

How could I stop
numbering bones?

Cabin Coffin

This is a bosun's game: imagine a ship foundering on an unexpected rock. In this catastrophe, one cabin of the hundreds on board, presumably a below water line cabin, is sealed off and two passengers perish in it – Cabin Coffin.

Prayer Before Embarkation
(I devised this months before setting off
and recite it silently on the gangplank.)

To any God of any Human:
Bless the ship that we sail on.
If we drown before we arrive,
we pray to you our work to save.

I see the smile disappear from my physicist's face. Here, in this rising water, we are a society of twin souls, physicist and poet, a very special category in Cabin Coffin's soul-searching game. Passengers have no idea they have been chosen as contestants. Well, we know now. The brine inside our door is like a meat-eater's breath dangling its sinews over our vegetarian hands.

Yet there is a gold burnishing the diminishing room: is it the thing we've grasped that is almost in the world's grasp? Has it steamed off the physicist in his last fear, like last words? Or off me, like a poem, all lyric glitter bubbling?

So we are the Crystalliers and this is Cabin Coffin. The *S.S. Eschatology's* awarding body – there will surely be an award – will make an irritable statement that their awardees offer more than merely not to be. Their council will cite my physicist's passion. They will say – He Showed Us the Human Face of Science.

Which is now under water

They will say, he taught us this: wisdom is deciding between good and bad data.

But there. Now I'm underwater myself. And in swims *Sorry*.

Aquarius

Our state room is polyphonic with *Sorry*
since experiments and poems
have not yet cooled the warming world.

     I tell him:
'You are balancing buckets –

your shoulders carry the burden of two poles:
        nurturing sun
        damaging sun.

     I see you
studying deserts,

divining light like water,
      freeing it for us,
       called to sense the sands…

     And then, Aquarius,
you'll save our age from us.'

In Which He Rejects the Image of a Saviour

Ouch –

So I say, 'How about we are both experimental philosophers?'
to take the awe
down a notch.

In deflection, he proposes a riddle:

'The riddle of the quantum well solar cell:

What is patient as a stone?
What stays and goes?
What saves us after fission, coal, and gas betray us?

Answer?'

'Fine crystal.'

Debate on a Private Deck

He refers me back to the jib of
my job and I jib at that:
'Riddles? That's Victorian verse.'

'Physics has got holier since the Victorians,' he says,
'less *applied* in the public consciousness.
Mine is applied.'

'Oh well
that word "holy"
sounds like "holey".'

What I will always remember of his words are these:

'The so-called holes
in a solar cell
are positive particles.'

About What You Said Yesterday

'Also,' I say next day, 'the word   "mechanics"
suggests   "here is
                    machinery"

a no soul   quantum hole…'

He likes that.
'…suggested by the first use of quantum mechanics:
        the big bad bomb.
        It delayed solar cells
        and silicon chips.'

Lost in Concert

Talk is so tiring, so tiring, each day decked
with its long planks of verbality.

At a concert in the ship's theatre,
a boy's T-shirt reads: *Kickin Seaview,*

the pianist grips the adagio,
suspends his one-drop note,

and my physicist falls asleep, undone.
Felt-tips cascade as far as our feet.

He shakes in his sleep
as Grieg's concerto shakes, shakes, shakes.

The Medium and the Dream of Mission

another night of onboard entertainment where my physicist falls asleep

I'm going to come to you, you with the black
Jeans and dinner jacket.
That's an interesting combination we don't often see on board.
I'm cheeky, sir, I know it!

I've got a tall man and a tall woman here:
And they're telling me not to worry,
That you're catching a quick nap.
Are you his wife, lady sitting next to him?
Lady in the orange knitted vest?
No need to wake him.

They say that he stands up for what he believes.
Is this his mother, about a head taller than me?
Yes? Was she anxious? Loving but anxious?
Does that make sense to you?

And she wants you both to know they are all together
And could you tell him they are waiting for him?
And they are so proud of him, not just his...
I'm getting the word mission or vision or belief?
Does that make sense?

Your life is hard now, I see, a struggle but you are strong.
All their strength is in you and though he is asleep –
No, that is OK, people sleep in their insights –

Do you have a small dog?
No. Say no, if it doesn't make sense. I can only say
What I'm given. Perhaps a large cat. No?
Do you feel about his mission,
Do you feel his mission is a dependent animal?

If I was writing that down, I'd put a capital M:
Mission and you can hear that capital, sir, though you're asleep.

You have now gone to the spirit plane, this is unusual –
Everyone here must believe in what they believe –
And I don't have to get help because you're also on earth
And your previous wife is saying it's not your time –

Does this make sense to you?
Your Mission has not gone with you to the astral plane.
They have taken your hand to lead your spirit back,
Back to your seat.
Of course, your body is still on the earth plane.
It has never left it.
Does that make sense?

You are opening your eyes
As you do every time you fall asleep in a theatre –
Cheeky, I know, sir! –
You're feeling the weight of your Mission and the people
Here with me though you can't see them now,
Now that you've woken up.

Do you feel it?

Yes!!!

An Idea for a Research Proposal Comes in the Night
and Reminds Me of His Marriage Proposal

In bed, he jack-knifes, brimming:
thought is testing him.
Darkness turns toward the sun,

and his mind, a faithful mountain,
gathers its leap,
kicks itself out of its sleep to be moved
from void to empyrean

where my ring's gold slides up
and down my ring finger, flight
on a monument to that
rhetorical question: my physicist's

proposal....

Clifftop Meeting, a Flashback

The Needles, Isle of Wight

I fell by cloud. The greys of sky were wool,
were stitches, millions of them, and they spooled
out birds and unseen fishes and the whole
what-have-you of control.

I breathed that stuff as I fell through the air,
into my nose and throat, lanolin and hair,
till my inside was purled and plained and scared.
Who will care

that like a filament of yarn, I spun,
was whirled, unfurled, and hung on needle bones.
Dive, I did, I dived and did I land
on ground-sun coloured sand?

Like a Carbon Offset

I wake one night, slipped ever so slightly in time
and think of the encomia we've heard:
'It is a great pleasure for me
to live in the era of such a Professor.' *[sweet!]*

'   .'   *[almost generic]*

'   .'   *[like a carbon offset]*

The Blessing

The words of encomia are precarious in our mouths
like sea inside our heads.

We take sun.

It gives itself to us.

Worlds of Wanwood

after 'Spring and Fall' by Gerard Manley Hopkins

i
O welcome interregnum on deck seven!
Children cartwheel and adults play seals in the pool.

ii
Young Claire, flowing in her handstands over to
lands where feet are bare
of virtue.

Though you think now, cartwheeling, you see best under,
perfect arcs blunder
from peak point

reversing. You've stammered growing, giving rise to
grand postures. Let no
one say no.

Know, unflaring down from higher ground, you are sharing
each fall with all soles
that labour.

iii
I sometimes see Keith when I see a child
fitting a long track together, grey plastic bars
into bridges, ramps and an end-stay, ease
a ship into a sling, releasing
the catch. Picking it up with splayed
fingers and thumb, careering it down air's wave,
crawling it across wet planks, hills
of tables. Hovering the ship
on the brink of a glazed rail.

Serious hand: thinking for smaller things.

A Hell of Saints

I've collected saints by the narrow definition.
The broad definition makes everyone a saint:
God rightly sees us that way, even the devil

who, my friend Paul told me when I was five,
playing on a small perfectly round green island
outside my house, stretches a person

till they crack and that's called torture
and we Catholics invented it. Once I could see hell
from my front doorstep, I wanted to watch

saints flourish. My friends, you'll know
saints are not my tribe. But now I have a collection.
Yes, it's motley. Two poets. An office worker.

A fabric designer (retired). My physicist.
Many humble, few proud, miracles worked.
The proof is in the joy. A hell of a saint

makes the presence of heaven in its absence

on this ark,
on these unbeatable waves.

Think Workers

    The ship of our time is no tree
with a yard arm, a mast. No walnut shell rocks us home.

    Planes charge across skies, leaves blowing
away from the branch. But we two travel water-earthed

in this swaying skyscraper of a carbon-saver.

    We think
    We think and talk
    We talk of thoughts

                We – what workers are this we –
                think – what work is not thought –

    Whose thought crosses:
        hours with days
        power with energy
        means with ends

Electricity Generation in Germany in a Typical April Week

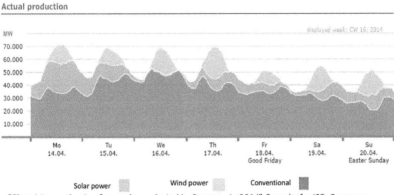

"Electricity production from solar and wind in Germany in 2014", Fraunhofer ISE, Germany

...while others say the sun doesn't shine enough,
it does.

It shines most powerfully

at the peak of our demand,
when we most need it –

the golden areas are small
but they peak

and peak
when we most need them.

Gold Standard

Outside, a feral surface.

     It hisses apart for our ship   seething and soothing

          the dry soles
that walk our way.

     One of us
            meditates

     on how to demonstrate linkage

       repeatableconsistentreproducedoverandover.

     The same one of us remarks on the glory of coincidence:

'Is sun gold
because, of all its photons,
golden ones
are the most plentiful?
Causal connection
or coincidence?'

'Coincidentally,
the energy of a golden photon
is just right for a solar cell
to operate most efficiently.'

                           No transcript of my response to this.

OK, Professor

Upcoming are the facts for government advisors:

Power is measured in the instant of its happening.

Energy is measured over a period.

Power transforms energy.

Power supply and power demand must always balance on the grid.

Power is the amount by which energy changes in a second.

The power of the sun turns nuclear energy from its core into the energy of sunlight.

Solar power arrives around the time of day when power demand is highest.

The foot that kicks the ball must kick it when it comes.

It's power we consume.

It's power the sun generates.

OK, Professor

Surprise Kiss

Dolphins leap
out of the black-tipped waves
fins airstruck
up
drop
back to the still-filled sea.

Beyond our mahogany rail, porpoises –
on deck seven people are guessing 'Porpoises!' –
leap in their pairs and
black
shines, every colour.

In the shade of a lifeboat –
Quick!
Kiss!

and each synecdoche gives up
its part.

Since his arms clutch me in
love, he has me now.

Since his arms clutch me in
fear and he pushes my mouth so
explosively in that salty air, a syll-
able enjambed, half fall-

ing
to a lower line, toss-
ing up the word that works for it-
self, love, and since that

has dis-
lodged my innate amorality and, though
force from anyone else would not show
love, he has me now.

Dolphin on the Wing

So, bored brain,
could you be a sun-sought electron

excited
into power by a photon of light?

Swifts swooping
for flying food go on and on looping.

Dolphins soar
out of ocean to a wind-throned feather.

Yes. Our call
is to outswim them in this dry well.

What We Know

One midnight we pass
one hundred and fifty miles east of the *Titanic*.
She lies in deep waters.

Good Captain Roston steamed his ship *Carpathia*
through an iceberg field to find survivors.
The children were lifted on board in mail sacks.
The designer and the owner of unsinkability
saved no-one. Nor did Jack the telegrapher,
who ignored warnings of ice fields.

Other boats knew.

Ten seconds from touch, that huge ship filled with water.

Other boats knew
and warned
and were not listened to.

'So' – I slip in while he ponders tea parties
and fur coats that warmed the swells –
'it was that subtle ship of electrons, Captain Roston,
who rescued the drowning world back then.'

My physicist wakes up his computer.
Opens his file of graphs.
Begins an analysis.

Becalmed

a prehumous song

Darklight, darklight
we rest in you
remembering
we are not two

wherever dark
is light. Dark shines
on every line
in scripts of mine

and darklight, though
no human sight
can catch you, you
illuminate

his cell, his leaf.
Communicate
your powers. We need
you day and night.

Darklight, darklight,
our light, our dark,
if there is more
for us to sense,

shake out your grains
of star and park
the continents.
So let us stare

becalmed offshore.
So let him be.
But if your love
take him, take me.

Salt

For I am saline in huge quantities and charge the sea and with me he is
        marine and submarine.
For he is saline in huge quantities and charges the sea and with him I am
        marine and submarine.

For with me he is rock.
For with him I am rock.

For he is of the earth and with him I am scattered on defeated ground and
        buried deep and dug up.
For I am of the earth and with me he is scattered on defeated ground and
        buried deep and dug up.

For with him I am taxed.
For with me he is taxed.

For I am the glittering covenant and with me he is promised and faithful.
For he is the glittering covenant and with him I am promised and faithful.

For with me he is shaken and devoured.
For with him I am shaken and devoured.

For he is spilt and thrown over the world's shoulder and with him I am
        elevated and dashed and I am called lucky.
For I am spilt and thrown over the world's shoulder and with me he is
        elevated and dashed and he is called lucky.

For with him I am common.
For with me he is common.

For I might hurt the heart and the channels of the heart and with me
        he is fearsome to inappropriate lovers.
For he might hurt the heart and the channels of the heart and with him
        I am fearsome to inappropriate lovers.

For with me he is salaried and rich enough.
For with him I am salaried and rich enough.

For he is a solar scientist who can focus the sun onto salt through ten
                    thousand mirrors and with him I am powered.
For I am a solar scientist who can focus the sun onto salt through ten
                    thousand mirrors and with me he is powered.

For with him I am preserved.
For with me he is preserved.

Transtraditional Atlantic

We cross
the Atlantic, on a ship that insists

on its past.
Let's take the future. The last

morning
we whistle: a new graph! Is it *now*,

the turning
from fossil to solar cell fuel?

These lovers'
crossings burn devotion.

Such solar affairs aren't long.

Physicist, is it over?

Poet, how strong
a voyage have you sung

to power-fill an ocean?

Margins, Curled

gingerly between light and hydropower,
run
till horizons claim the sun.

Notes

p.11   *Rapture Physics is the branch of science that believes this: just before the imminent catastrophic loss of our species, some few chosen physicists have been gathered up into a heaven of knowledge. The special task of those physicists, while waiting out the end times, is to define the smallest particles dancing in the first nanosecond of the universe and in the head of the last pin.

p.18 *CERN: Conseil Européen pour la Récherche Nucléaire

p.24 'Abstract' is lineated from John G. Jenkin, *Physics in Perspective*, Vol 13, issue 2, June 2011, pp128-145

p.45 Aquarius is the sign of the water carrier. *The Aquarius* is a special-purpose ship chartered by SOS Méditerranée, a European maritime and humanitarian organisation, and Médecins Sans Frontières to rescue migrants and refugees in trouble at sea.

BIBLIOGRAPHY
Barnham, Emeritus Professor Keith, *The Burning Answer, A User's Guide to the Solar Revolution*, Weidenfeld and Nicolson, 2014

Lightning Source UK Ltd.
Milton Keynes UK
UKHW011002140222
398659UK00001B/88